Even Lost Souls
Need to Laugh

By Joyce Cannon Yi

Front cover: "Man in a Wicker Chair" by TC Cannon.,1975, oil and
acrylic on canvas, 72 x 60 in.
Back cover: Photo of Author, Joyce Cannon Yi, sitting in wicker chair
recreation of "Man in a Wicker Chair"
Interior sketches by: TC Cannon.
Page 92: "Woman at the Window" by TC Cannon, 1975, oil on
canvas, 46.5 x 40 in.

Edited by: Joyce Cannon and Marsha Chotiner
Technical assistance: Fritz von Coelln

Printed in the United State of America

ISBN: 9781687224545
Cannon Yi Publishing

This book is dedicated to all the Lost souls everywhere. May the path you travel lead you to the place that can make you laugh once more.

Even Lost Souls Need to Laugh

How can I find myself again? How can I be happy and laugh when I cannot even love myself? Even lost souls need to laugh.

How many souls are lost. How many cling to the past but not see the present, not realizing that the present can alter the future.

Maybe in some ways we are all lost souls waiting to be found. Each searching for that certain someone who makes us yearn for a long-ago time. A time when we could smell the season of spring. When we could smell the wet dirt after a rain. When we could smell the beauty of a new day and what it holds. A time when we were not alone.

I fear my mind will not hold the memories that made me laugh. I fear the memories will go down into the pit of hell with other lost souls.

I live alone. This broken spirit has no hope of love to quiet this mind. I try not to think about my situation. But it can be difficult when you feel the need to just go ballistic.

I guess I will crawl into the darkness of the night and try to watch the darkness slip into daylight. Maybe then, this lost soul can smile even if I can't laugh.

Table of Contents

Family

Friends

Love

Potpourri

Acknowledgments

I would like to thank Fritz von Coelln for all of the
time he spent getting this book together. Without his patience,
knowledge and that brilliant mind this book would not have been
made. It may have challenged more so than other projects but if so
he never once let on that it did.

I would like to thank Marsha Chotiner for all of the help
she contributed to this project. Thank you so much
Marsha for all of her time and help. She is one of
A kind.

Family

Soldier Boy

Soldier boy so brave and noble, enlisting in a not so noble war, not knowing if you would return.

You traded in your western boots for combat boots, your jeans and blue work shirt for a uniform of green, got a haircut and off to jump school you went.

Still a boy in many ways; just out of your teens, you were sent to the distant shores of Vietnam. Vietnam in all of its beauty in some ways, but during war, an ugly place of desolation and smell of death.

The boy I called brother came back a man: a man, who was shattered, dark, and brooding. Who knows what misery one sees in war? How it changes a gentle being into his own worst enemy.

The "demons of war" may have taken your smile and laughter, but they didn't take your soul.

That soul belonged to God, whom you served and loved. The God that said "Come home soldier and be with me. You served your time in hell, now come home to me."

So you left again. This time the God of Gods wanted another beautiful soul to serve him in Heaven.

RIP Soldier Boy...You were always my hero.

Expectations

Come go with me.

We will walk along the Washita River and throw rocks
trying to make them skip along the water.
We will sit and down some rabbit beer.

You will tell me of your latest dream of wanting to have
your paintings shown in Paris, London and New York.

I will tell you my desire to write the Great American
Novel. We both laugh and know that will never
happen just the Coors talking.

In reality we watch the sun go down, and
drink a few more brewskies.

Yes! In reality one of us will have our dream
come true I guess we know who that is, don't we?

His paintings are shown all over the world
including Europe as well as other countries and in New
York and these United States of America.

Dreams do come true. Too bad he didn't live to see his
dream come true.

The other one is yet to come...Maybe...just maybe one
just has to be persistent and unduly hopeful.

The Strength of a Grandmother

She looked into his blue eyes and blushed. He looked into her brown eyes and smiled. The blue eyed blonde Irishman and the raven haired native girl fell in love at the mission school they attended. They married and had five children whose ages were two years apart.

They were happy for a while, but sometimes the heart feels the need to wander. So the Irishman left with someone else he thought would quell the wanderlust in his heart.

The native beauty had to dig inside her inner strength and feed and raise her children alone. Wood to cut, gardens to tend, vegetables to can. Times were hard at first.

A flu epidemic hit and took many lives. Her youngest, a son was not expected to live. Men came and sang their native songs, from their voices to the Creator's ears. Eventually the boy recovered. God had other plans for this boy. He grew up to be the father of Joyce Cannon and Tee Cee Cannon.

One day the Irishman showed up and asked to be taken back. Not wanting to travel that road again, she sent him on his way. Charlie Ira Cannon was a long-gone lover who was no longer welcome in her world.

Grace Two Hatchet Cannon was a pioneer woman whose strength was challenged many times. She walked a dark path of failure in her marriage, but from failure came a physical and mental energy to rival any man.

I doubt if there are women today who could raise five children alone, including myself. I am proud to carry her name, Day-ma-pi-ah, translating to "Pleading with her" or "Pleading for her".

The only thing that could defeat this strong woman was time and Parkinson's disease.

She passed in the house where she raised her children. The house full of love and memories. She did not die a lonely soul. Her children as well as her brothers and sisters were with her to the very end.

This strong woman left this world with one last good-by smile to all.

Grandpa's Chair

The old man sits in his chair. No one else is allowed to sit there.

The grandchildren gather around and he tells them stories to make them laugh and others to make them wonder in amazement with open mouths.

I was told he was a great worrier at one time. He provided meat for the whole campground. He fought bravely in battle against the enemy.

One day he left and never came back. Mom told us to not sit in his chair.   Just because we can't see him doesn't mean he is not there.

When I became a teenager, I would pull up a chair and talk to grandpa. Tell him about my day. I told him that after I marry and have a son I will name him "Roars Like Thunder" after him.

Do my eyes deceive me? Call it wishful thinking, but I think I saw him in the chair smiling at me.

Then he disappeared, back into his chair.

The man, my hero, still sits in his chair, watching.

That Last Day

Sitting here thinking of you. Wondering what was your last thought, on that last day. Did you think of me and say to yourself, "perhaps I should call her."

When you went into town for your last meal, did you enjoy it more, or did you not even give it a thought

What was your last earthly vision? Perhaps a tree. Did you see the moon on rocks? Did you hear the singing of the wind out on the desert, or the echo of death saying "come home, time for you to come home."

We both knew you would not be around in your earthy shell for long. So you made up for it by living and loving hard and fast.   You touched a lot of hearts and in doing so, made a lot of friends.

I hope being the gentle soul you were, you went gently into the night with only one regret. That you didn't tell everyone how much you loved and appreciated them.

Somehow we know...we know

Be Like a Mirror

A telephone awakens me. I answer and it's you wanting to talk to me, like you did as a teen and as a soldier. You ask if I am happy. Doing the best I can. Trying not to let people use me. Be like a mirror," he said. "Then there will be two of you fighting for what is right."

You sing a song to me, "Early Morning Rain," that you know is my favorite.

When you are finished singing you tell me to stay strong. That's why I chose you to be a part of my life. I will, I answered. Good night he said and hung up.

After a while the phone rings again and awakens me. What is happening? Then I realize that the first call was only a dream. It seemed so real.

I wish you would call me so that I can tell you how you burst upon the art scene and brought tears to the eyes of many who saw your works for the first time. You seemed to explode all at once. You inspired many new artists.

But then again, I guess wherever you are, you are aware of that.

Bonding with Papa

Come with me my father said. We went to the storm
cellar in our back yard and sat down on
the top of it.

He lit a cigarette and we talked about nothing of
importance.   He asked about school, who were my
friends, what was my teacher's name.

After a while he passed me the cigarette and I took a
puff.

Some more small talk. Passing the cigarette back and
forth until we finished it. Was this his way of bonding
with me? Did he not know what to say to me?

We finished the cigarette and went back to the house.
Just the two of us.

He asked me not to tell my mother that he let me
smoke. And I didn't! Until the next week. She bawled
me out but said nothing to my father.

One of the memories I have of my father. After all, I
shared my first cigarette with my father at the ripe old
age of six years old.

Pai-doung-u-day

(Standing inside the sun)

Years ago the Kiowas were having a Pow Wow. One of the dancers looked up and saw the outline of a man inside the sun. Pai-doung-u-day which translates to "Standing Inside the Sun". Many people of generations that have passed since then, I imagine, have carried that name.

Most Native children are given a Native name when they are born. Tee Cee Cannon was given that name, when he was born.

The name appeared to fit him as he was always so smart, and stood out in a crowd.

Today that light still shines brightly to all who knew and loved him as well as to the younger generation of artists whom he influenced.

Who knows...perhaps one day I will look up at the sun and see an outline of a man. A familiar individual who I grew up with: my brother Tommy Wayne (Tee Cee) Cannon, paying homage to his name.

One can hope. Stranger things have been known to happen.

Windows

Windows to look in or out of.

Look out at the children playing, a couple going for a walk with their dog Maddie to who knows where. To the store, the neighbors, or just to exercise. Perhaps to find that dusty country road where they feel the contentment of a long-ago childhood.

I look in a window and see a family laughing: all together, joined as a loving unit. I look in another window and see a man...alone. He cannot comprehend the loneliness that comes with old age and offspring that are too involved in their own lives to spend time with, or make a telephone call to him. Old age can be a demonic, unkind existence.

I look in your eyes...the windows to your soul and see a peacefulness. A calm that makes me feel euphoric. If only others could see the beauty of your soul.

Then the world would delight in the same peace and calm I experience when I look into your soul.

Massacre at Sand Creek

I heard the thunder of horse's hoofs. Then I hear the anguished screaming of women and children.

I step outside my tipi and see mutilated bodies everywhere. Women and children with ears and fingers cut off. How can this be? You said Sand Creek would be my home. Now you want to kill everyone so you can have it back?

Only old men, women and children who cannot put up much of a fight are in camp. I notice my child is silent in my arms. He will sleep the sleep of eternity.

A soldier with a sabre drawn rides toward me. I look at him but do not run. I keep walking toward him carrying my beautiful child.

I walk and keep walking toward this cowardly bastard. He raises his sabre, but I do not raise my arms to protect myself, nor do I run. I will not give him that pleasure.

Then his sabre comes down on me.

Then darkness.

Now my child and I will live forever in the land where my ancestors were sent when they also could fight no more.

Dreams of Real Life and More

What do babies dream? Cotton candy clouds, a favorite stuffed animal.

What do you as a teenager dream about? A cute girl with dimples and curly hair who stole your heart.

As a soldier sleeping in a bunk bed during war? Dreaming of going home once more. Some fellow gladiators will not make it home. Peace comes at a high price.

You as a husband sleeping in the arms of your wife? Happiness galore. But nothing lasts forever, not even love.

A single man once more who stays up late, painting way into the night to finish a painting which you will name "Tosca". Not knowing it will be your last. Sweet dreams of any artist who finishes another work of art.

Driving down Old Pecos Road the desert is beautiful, like a lake of sand filled with lizards, snakes, flowers and cacti.

Creatures that live and love in their desolate surroundings.

Getting sleepy. Very sleepy.

Suddenly you awaken and look at the entity holding you. A warm golden glow of peacefulness and love come over you.

God has called you home where your spirit will live forever...

In GOD'S perfect love for you.

16

Gone but Not Forgotten

He played guitar and harmonica. Mostly Bob Dylan—
his idol.

Music to him was like a virus that held on to him and
didn't let go. I wish we could all be in tune with the
songs and music he left behind.

This talented individual who could get people up on the
dance floor.

He appeared to me in a dream and told me he was
writing songs and singing with the other Tom (Petty).

They wrote a song called "Gone But Not Forgotten".
He sang a verse for me. I was happy he made a new
friend to jam with.

Yes! The both of you, Tommy Cannon and Tom Petty
left your fingers and hand prints, on every musical
instrument, on every song and on every painting you
touched.

You may be gone, but not forgotten.

Fade in And Fade Out

I stood looking at the plowed cotton field. I could
see myself as a child picking the cotton, weighing it,
emptying the sack and out to the field again. At the
young age of six I was out in the fields picking
cotton. A hard life for one so young.

My parents got the money I made. At the age of ten
I complained, so they gave me my wages and I
bought clothes. My father thought I would spend it
foolishly. Even at that young age I was a responsible
person.

Sometimes at the end of the day, your hands
would be cut from the piercing of the cotton bolls
on your hands. Also a back that ached like it was
going to break.

It was hard work but times were hard. I needed
socks and a sweater to protect me from the
Oklahoma winter. Also some comic books to keep
me from boredom.

I walked down to the creek, took off my shoes and
waded in the cool water. After a while I put my
shoes back on and walked up to the field again. It
was not a happy time and I had to grow up at an
early age.

Now! I will walk away from those memories of hard times, but keep the ones like shelling pecans as a snack while I read the comic books over and over again.

For once let me be a child

"If You Give Me A Nickel"

If someone asked a favor of my father, he would say. If you give me a nickel."

Toward the end of his life I was unable to be with him so we spoke by telephone. We reminisced about the good old days. He laughed, I cried. I knew this would be the last time we would talk.

Knowing he was tired I told him I would let him rest. "I love you," I told him. He said "I love you too." I was happy that in our later years we were able to get past the hostility that was once there and enjoy each other's company.

The following Thursday I could not sleep so I got up and went to the living room and sat in the dark. The telephone rang at 6:00 am. I knew what it was. He had passed in the night.

Did he stretch forth his fragile hand to the angel who was sent to bring him home? His soul would leave this prison of pain that encompassed his body, and he would be well once more. He would be reunited with the person he missed and loved more than anyone...his son.

On his casket at his funeral I saw a nickel in a box. I asked around but no one seemed to know where it came from.

Did an angel leave it there to say my father was watching out for me? I don't know, but the next time I see him I will ask where that nickel came from. He will probable look at me and say...

"I'll tell you, If you give me a nickel."

Take My Hand

I was given a quarter to take you to the movies
Saturday night in Anadarko, Okla. What was our
mother thinking? A seven-year old and a four-year
old. It was a block and a half to the theater. I took
your hand to walk you across the street to protect
you. We had three busy streets to cross. Busy
Saturday night in those days.

When we got to the theater I had a nickel left from
the quarter. I bought you a candy bar.

You smiled all through the movie. I don't think you
understood the movie. I guess you felt grown up.

I held your hand again as we went back to where
our mother was sitting and visiting with other
women.

Now I have an empty room in my heart and wish
you could reach down and take my hand.
Something to quell this grief in my heart. Grief sits
with me when I recall the memories of you. Two
siblings who leaned on each other and grew to be
the best that they could be.

Someday when we meet again and you come
running to greet me, after a hug, you will take my
hand to show me around.

Two children again holding hands again. To protect and show love for each other. This time I will be the one with a smile on my face, just as you did when we were children.

Yes I will, I certainly will.

Footsteps

Trying hard to remember my first footsteps. Hard to remember when you are nine months old. Did I fall and cry? More than likely I got up and tried again.

Listening to my mother's footsteps resonating in sound at a very rapid pace. Coming into the room and yelling at me for one reason or other. Like the child I was, who had known mostly sorrow with her, I say nothing. We sit in the same room saying nothing. I wonder if love was blind or so distant inside of her not to feel anything for the child she bore.

We sit in silence.

Listening to my brother's footsteps. His steps are long in stride. He enters the room and we talk awhile. How I admire the talent and charisma this individual possesses. He takes out a pad and starts to sketch. Who knows what the image will be. I ask no questions of him.

We sit in silence.

I never heard my father's footsteps. Was it psychological knowing that he was hardly at home. He was restless and not a family person. How can you hear footsteps that are not there?

Sometimes you have to open your heart, even a little to let the love of a child enter and bring a feeling of love like no other.

Later In life he sits and watches T.V.

We sit in silence.

As an adult listening to my footsteps, they burn and hurt. But, I persevere and take the walk. I walk away from all the hurt and sadness of the past. Soon my feet do not burn or hurt at all. Walking away to a new life of happiness and pleasure.

I was not going to live my life in silence.

Listening to my husband's footsteps as he walks into the room. They are slow, but sturdy and strong. He smiles and sits down next to me. We talk and reminisce about our youth when we were a young callow couple. We made many memories together.

This person who sauntered into my life and left his foot prints on my heart. I never had to deal with anything pertaining to unfaithfulness, neglect or abuse. A thoughtful person he is, a lucky person I am. Now we sit in our golden years laughing and happy.

We do not sit in silence.

Friends

I Will Write You a Poem

God gave us friends for a reason.
Friendship is food to our body.
It strengthens and feeds us when needed.
It gives us love when we are lonely and sad.

I consider myself lucky to have a piece of
my friend's heart.

I will write a poem for you and you will carry
it in your memory forever.

     Or

Until you make another friend.

Quiet Memories of a Guitar

Here I stand leaning against a wall. People walk by, some stopping to look, others glancing and walking on.

Why am I here? Where is my master? The man who took me in his arms and softly strummed my strings and played Dylan. A tear would water his eye and roll down his cheek. Perhaps memories of a lost love that cannot escape his mind or heart. The songs he wrote were skillfully written, even in a confused mind when the song had no words. He rocked hard. He was a rocker. Yes he was.

And then he was gone...I never saw him again.

I was put in my case and left there for so long. Loneliness can be a prison.

Now my new master, who adores me, let some people take me away and put me on display for people to see and enjoy at my former master's art show. Here I stand.

One day I will have a new master. It will be a two-way love affair. The music that will come from my strings will bring a smile or a tear to their eye. Music does that to you.

Looking back I had the best in masters. The most talented, creative individuals who played like the best.

Now excuse me while in my quiescence this guitar gently weeps for lost love and memories past.

Relationships

Some relationships...friends/acquaintances are like a puzzle with a missing piece. Not whole. Some grow over the years, others grow apart and one moves on.

A thought of leaving one behind. Creating a void that can hopefully be filled again with someone new. I hope I leave a happy memory of myself when I am gone. A memory to make one smile.

Then again I can open the door, and if you feel like entering, some day we may call each other friend...a REAL FRIEND of emotions, not a false friend of words... or maybe not. I will have it no other way.

Enter the door or slam it shut. If the time has come and gone and cannot be made whole...so be it.

The lost piece to the puzzle can be found and made whole again. Or we can stop looking for that missing piece and wave good-by forever.

False Face

Is your face a mask for the surface of false smiles
                    Or
the sincere look of friendship?

If I was to leave today would I be a memory worth
remembering
                    Or
a forgotten being in that orbit of endless beings that
circulate in your black space of nobodies long forgotten?

Call me friend or don't call me anything.

                    For
I can see through the mask,
through the fakeness of the fake smile.

                    For
you see I also am a being who can see with eyes,
feel with emotions and think with mind.

There is a hurting in my heart because I
gave my best and it was not enough.

My heart may be hurting yet
I will survive because ...

I will not allow you to quell the spirit in me with
your false smiling mask of counterfeit emotions.

Friendship in a Glass

My friends and I were talking about
friendship and what we meant to each
other.

I said that a relationship/friendship can
be like an hour glass.

The sand runs out and the glass is empty.
You can turn the glass over and let the
empty glass fill up again, or you can leave
the glass empty.

That is your decision.

Will we be friends full of life or an entity
that becomes empty and life is minus
one less person in your life.

Choose wisely so your glass will always
be full.

Lonesome Tears

lonesome tears ... let them flow

let the false friends who never cared
the cold uncaring parent
the unkind remarks of your peers
flow into that boundless three-dimensional place
called Hades

let the lonesome tears flow into your pillow tonight
let the tears release you from all who have broken your
heart
let the tears flow

let the lonesome tears flow

shit

tomorrow you will wake up and wonder why you cried
those lonesome tears

Scripted words

How was your week-end... do you really care?
What are you doing this week-end...you have
no interest in what I will be doing

Hope you are fine...do you really want me to be OK

Scripted words that mean nothing to you
Words you don't even realize you are saying
Words that just come out naturally

I have a heart that feels and can break into a million
pieces with scripted words

I have eyes that can shed a million tears because of
your scripted words

I love you... then you turn around and walk away
I miss you...but you never call

Hell

I think I will go to the nearest bar, sit down, order a drink
and ask the bartender, "What's new" I don't really want
to know how your week-end was... as if I really care or
why did you become a bartender... I have no interest

I guess I can be as scripted as the next person

Forgiveness

Some people say I am immature. Others say I am
sarcastic but not sardonic. I concur. My wit is such
that I can bring a smile to a face or a stoic look that
says, "Grow up. Don't be a loser."

I am who I am. I do my own thing, and some people
accept me as I am and are my friends. Others who do not
accept me are entitled to their opinion, and I can respect
that. We do not all think the same.

Some people say, "I love you dearly," while others
have little regard for me...which is satisfactory to me. I
love God, my family and friends.

My heart is open to all who want to enter or to
others who want to leave.

If you leave and want to come back you are welcome and
embraced in a gracious manner.

Forgiveness can be hard. But if you come back and cause
me pain again my heart will have a lock on it and be
closed to you forever.

If you are sincere and trustworthy in your friendship with
me...then I say to you, "Come into my heart my friend."

"Welcome home."

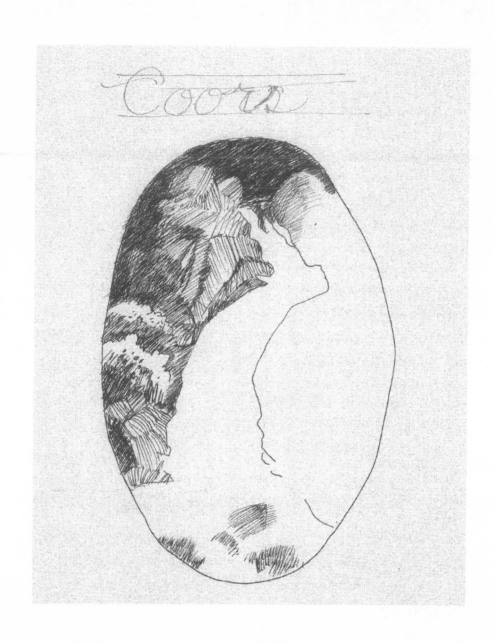

Rabbit Beer

Got my Rabbit beer, Vienna sausages and crackers
Funny how as adults we still enjoy our childhood
snackers

Not answering the door
I have a song to write
Most surely must get it done tonight

Mind is blank and deceives me
The words I need are absentee

Open another Rabbit beer and think
Did this sluggish mind shrink
That's what I think
Think...Think...Think...

What the heck I will open the door
I will invite my friends in once more
They can have my sausage, crackers and other snackers
But leave my beer alone
They all let out a groan

    Hell

Since they are already here
Why not give them each a beer
But no hanging from the chandelier
You hear?

The Past

Saying "I'm sorry" when you are wrong can make a difference in a relationship.

Do not hold on to the past. Move on and make a happier life.

The past will always be a ghost lurking. Forget the unkind ghost and concentrate on the present time.

The present is a time of change and making wonderful memories.

Memories so that in the future you can look back on the now...present time, and say "darn, that time in the past was a good time in my life."

"I'm glad I have no unkind scars from that time. Only wonderful memories."

So! Will you have wonderful memories or an unkind ghost lurking in the past?

Billy The Blue Leg Crow

Billy the blue leg crow sits on the telephone wire and sings his song. Caw, Caw, Caw.

His partner, Daisy, soon flies in and sits beside him.

Billy flies down and picks up a seed and flies back to the wire and gives it to her. Is this his way of saying I love you?

She accepts the seed and also sings the song. Caw, Caw, Caw. Is she saying, "I want to be with you"? Gee I wish I understood crow.

I watch awhile and listen to their singing.

After awhile Daisy flies away and Billy, the blue leg crow, also flies away.

Maybe tomorrow they will fly away together and live in happiness and sing together for the rest of their lives.

What a wonderful life story that would be.

After all, who says crows can't fall in love?

Nomad

You told me you loved me, but I have to say good-by.
I can't stay and be enclosed in someone's mental and
physical world.

I leave you with all that I have...memories.
Some to make you happy and some to make you sad.
I'm a drifter who must comprehend what this celestial
body called earth can present to this restless, craving
adventurous nomad. Perhaps it's a trait that I inherited
from my ancestors, the Kiowa.

Don't cry for me. Don't think badly of me. After all, a
memory can last a lifetime. Longer then an unforeseen
relationship that was not meant to be. A relationship
built on passion.

      Yet

If you are the answer to my needs...then I will see you
once again.

Love

Daydreams

One day a memory will come into your mind. Will you remember me with a smile on your face, or will it be a frown?

Either way I made an impression on you.

One day I realized that I wanted you and needed you.

One day you will realize that you needed me but didn't want me.

Some people love and need versus some people who need but don't love.

TSK TSK

Your needs are greater than your love. What a shame.

My mind is free and not bound by anything.
Can you say the same?

I Love You MORE

When I first looked into your eyes I saw kindness, and love. I tried to run because I knew my life would never be the same again. So I ran from you. Call it fate, or fortune, we were destined to be together.

I cannot imagine life without you.

The way you say "I love you more."

You took your vows seriously and took care of me though my illness and never complained. Not once did you complain.

I would describe you as a giver. You give a lot and expect or want nothing in return.

I would marry you all over again and never regret anything. I would take that journey with you and only you.

Because,

I love you MORE.

Two for One

Marie says that East Wheelock Street is quiet
and dark. She goes there in the rain. It is as empty as
she is today.

Marie in her emptiness stands in the rain ...
waiting for HIM hoping the spirit of HIM will come
walking down the dark rain soaked street that is
void of life.

Knowing he stepped on a mine in Vietnam
with nothing left of him but memories.
Still...this empty shell of a woman looks down the dark
empty street in the rain.

She struggles, but waits for the ghost of a
love of long ago, that will never come.
Perhaps, because his DNA that defined who
he was, has been scattered in a rice paddy
in Vietnam.

- This poem is based upon the first stanza that was written
  by TC Cannon.

The Violin is a Thing of Beauty

The notes can be soft and romantic
or entertaining on a foot stomping country
dance floor

It can bring back a memory of love long lost
or a smile to a face of a happy moment

The violin can be in the right hands...LOVE

Lovely to look at

Lovely to play

Yes! The violin is a thing to love

Whomever ends up with my violin. Treat it as though It
was one of the great loves of your life. I loved it and I, in
turn, pass this thing of beauty and love to you

Where Has My Beloved Gone

Gone like the cold wind that comes sweeping through your jacket on a winter day.

Gone like the years that have passed you by.

Gone like the laughter you once shared with friends at an amusement park.

Now I sit in my room with Mr. Darkness.

Darkness can be scary and horrifying to some.

Darkness can be calming and relaxing to others.

I dare not turn on the light and ruin this moment with my friend Mr. Darkness.

He has not left.

He is not gone.

One Day I Will Smile Again

I ran into you again after you left me two years before.
You said you wanted to start anew.

Do you have me in your heart now or do you just want
someone to spend the darkness with.

Will you make me smile again?

When you are far away do you think of me and lone for
me or do you look into another's eyes and tell her she is
the one.

I gave you more then you gave me. It still wasn't enough
for you.

My spiritual existence called life doesn't include
someone like you. I will weep but I will not die.

One day I will smile again.

Go now loser, to someone else who will listen in awe to
your insincere promises. Someone you can make smile,
until the next one comes along.

One day someone will deceive you, then leave you.
Then you will know what a broken heart feels like.

Then you will have no reason to smile.

Leaving Love Behind

You told me to leave...so I walked away with moistened eyes and trembling lips.

Where do I go I asked myself?
My friends say "suck it up".
The angels above will not show me the way.

I will go to this place called oblivion where other creatures like me with a wounded heart and a bruised ego go to die. I will go out into the desert to smoke and drink tea.

I watch as the Cacti hold hands and dance around.
A unicorn approaches me and nuzzles me.
I reach up and touch his horn. He runs away into the night never to be seen again.

Mr. Toad and Mr. Lizard just sit there and stare at me.
I ask Mr. Toad about his family.
He just stares with those protuberant eyes of his.

I will smoke and drink more tea.

The sand is like a crystal lake that shows the reflection of the moon. A lake without boats.
But with fish that swim by looking up at me as if to say, "jump in the water's fine."

I sense it is time for me to sleep.

I will reach up and grab some stars from the Milky Way, and cover myself with a blanket of stars. I will lay my head on a pillow of dreams.

Dreams will seep into this mass of brain that controls all thoughts and consciousness. Hopefully in my dreams a loved one will come visit me, hang out, and counsel me on my sorrowful situation.

In the morning, I will awaken, dust the sand off of my clothes and hair and say good bye to Mr. Toad who is still staring at me.

Yes! I will walk away from you, but I will not walk away from love.

I will not be blind nor deaf to love again. My soul will not be deflated.

I will dust not only my clothes off but the memory of you and your vitriolic being. Each day that passes takes me further away from you in memory.

Some day you will not even be a memory.

Walk Slowly

In life we walked...side by side...not one in front of the other, but side by side...partners.

Life handed us some ups and downs, but we prevailed and overcame the difficult situations together.

When the time comes when one of us leaves to go to the other side, it will be sorrowful and full of grief for the one left behind.

If I am the first to take that journey to the other side without you, I will walk the road very slowly. I will keep looking back to see if you are behind me, following me. They say a moment on the other side is months even years on this side. I would hope that you live a long life. Until then I will walk slowly waiting for you.

Perhaps I will sit on a rock and play with a squirrel. Then the tears will flow because I will miss my partner. A butterfly will land on my cheek and brush away the tears not wanting me to be sad. It will tickle my nose until I smile again. The sadness and loss will be great, but I will keep walking slowly, looking back, watching for you.

Then when I finally see you ...my heart will feel joyful again. One cannot go back on that road only forward, but I can wait for you to catch up.

When you see me you will come running to me, smiling and take me in your arms ...embracing me. Both of us will have tears, but also gladness. You will take me by the hand, and finally we will walk that road together to the other side.

Side by side... together just like we did in real life...

Partners.

Never to Be Again

A smile from across the room.
Deep set eyes that sparkle and flirt.
A dimpled chin that makes me sigh.

You cross the room, take me by the hand and ask if I
wanted to go outside to the patio and see the moon.

Then

Touching me lovingly with soft finger tips.
Running your finger over my mouth.
A gentle kiss on the neck.
A soft whisper in the ear that causes a blush.

Then suddenly a moan. Oh! Oh! Oh!
Yes! Yes! He answers.
No! No! My leg...
It has a cramp.

Darn it! I know I should have had a banana this morning.
Now that moment is lost.
Never to be again.

Moving On

I always knew the time would come when we would say good-bye...I just didn't think it would be so painful. I know what a broken heart feels like.

The agony and suffering one endures is lifelessness in its own state.

The dark path ventured alone. The sleepless nights thinking and pondering what went wrong.

I must forget and try to heal my scarred broken heart. So I will travel the road of life without you and someday you will be history...a forgotten being in a well of human species who chose to experience life with another.

I will smile again, I will enjoy life again, I will do it with a mended heart and in a state of contentment and happiness.

After all...we must experience sadness and misery to appreciate the exhilaration and contentment that comes with moving on and finding new loves.

My broken heart will mend, memories will fade. I will be far removed from your life forever....

   Mr. Heart Breaker.

You Made My Heart Smile

When I first saw you my heart smiled. The cute blonde boy with the cupid bow lips.

When we started talking, it was if we had known each other forever. Perhaps in another lifetime. Maybe we strolled down a street in Spain and held hands.

In this lifetime you gave me rides home after class. After a while we started dating and love blossomed. San Francisco was our playground.

Yet, sometime people make mistakes and things change. I don't blame you for leaving me. You took one last look at me, got on your motorcycle and you rode out of my life and heart.

Now at night I can hear the wind whistle your name. I reach out to touch you but the wind just moves on. I watch the shadows on the trees and other night Images and wonder if you also think of me.

Is it normal to love? After all it can bring sadness and heart ache. Do the butterflies in the stomach flutter away and leave you empty?

Yes! Love is worth it when it can make your heart smile even for a little while.

Yes it is. Yes it is.

The Richness of God

I am rich with the diamonds in the stars.
I have gold in the moon and sun.

Greenback dollar I do not need when I
have the green in all of nature: trees,
shrubs and grass.

The silver that sparkles on the water of
a lake makes me feel rich indeed.

But the richest thing in my life is the
love of almighty God who gave all of
this to me.

Walk Away, Walk Way

I watched as you walked away.
Trying to memorize every angle of your body.
The way your arms hung by your side, the
way you swayed when you walked.

I can't make you stay if you don't want to.
I can't make you love me if you don't feel it.

    Walk away, walk away

Years later when I hear the singing of the
wind at my window, and the wistfulness
gets the better of me, I will try to remember
how you left to find happiness elsewhere.

I will remember the way you walked away,
not even looking back. Too eager to distance
yourself from what you considered a burden
on your freedom and independence.

    Walk away, walk away

If you stayed, would we have been happy
together? We will never know because
you chose to walk away.

There are only sad songs to bring back the memories of what once was.

If you came to my door right now in all your handsomeness, I would look at you, smile and say:

Walk away, walk away.

I Drown in Your Eyes

Every time I look into your eyes, they are like
blue pools of water.

Water I am drawn to and drown in. Pools of
water that can be dangerous and pull me under.
Under to this thing called love.

Oh, what language eyes can speak. A language
without sound, but with all the words that life
can express. They speak their own language.

I will look into your eyes a bit longer until I
drown. Until I drown in those pools of love.

Until those beautiful pools speak back to me

Of love for me.

Another Snowflake

I love you...
I looked deeply into your brown eyes.
I pushed you away because you wronged me.

I pushed you far away so you found another.

Now as I sit here in my discontent, watching the
snow fall and mingle with other snowflakes that
make a carpet of white that will disappear. Just
as you disappeared from me.

Do I regret? Yes! I think of you all of the time,
but we cannot dwell on what might have been.
There will be another carpet of snow.

Another flake to land on me.

Then I will find the person who will be my present and
future.

Someone who will not disappear like the snowflakes.

Handsome Young Man on The Bridge

Every day they would meet on the wooden bridge. The handsome young man and the girl with the plump lips and infectious smile who stole his heart.

One day he said he was going away to a far-off land to serve his country.   She cried and ask him not to go. He said he had to go. It is a part of his heritage to be a warrior.

Now she goes alone, every day to the bridge, remembering...with sadness and misery...the handsome young man. She is also a victim of the far-off war.

She stands alone.

Waiting, Waiting.

One day he returns to her, but is different...a bit moody, dark and quiet. A changed man. She tries her best to help, but he won't listen. She cannot reach inside his brain that controls his thoughts to make him into the man he once was.

One day he went to the bridge and she was not there. Instead, there was a note telling him she was leaving. He is not the handsome young man she fell in love with. She has taken her pain and moved on.

Now the handsome young man goes to the bridge every day. Hoping, and wishing that one day he will see her come running to him with that same infectious smile that he fell in love with.

Until then the handsome young man stands alone on the bridge. A victim of a far-off war.

Waiting, Waiting.

Happiness in a Cup of Coffee (or Not)

He blows on his cup of coffee. His head down and his eyes with a sad look. I'm guessing his wife or girlfriend left him, or perhaps he lost his job.

He takes another gulp of his coffee and still no happy face. He just sits there and stares at the coffee in his cup.

Then he looks up and there she stands in the doorway. Their eyes meet and a smile breaks out on both their faces.

She goes to his table, sits down and they begin to talk. Both look happy. The coffee sits there in the cup getting cold, but they don't notice.

Let's face it men.

A hot woman will make you smile faster

than a hot coffee.

Champion Strut

You were quite the dandy
Very much eye candy

Champion rodeo star
as vain as they come

Someone who thinks he is
awesome and then some,
but is really "ho hum"

Someone who thinks no woman
will ever turn down otherwise
she will be on the receiving
end of an odious frown

He lights up his cigar
picks up his acoustic guitar
and heads for his car

He walks with that certain swivel
that only he can do...why he
walks like that I haven't a clue

Strutting past a group of girls he
hears a giggle. Him thinking they
like his wiggle. He smiles, then
walks away with that champion
strut, not knowing his pants
have a rip in the butt

64

Indian Lovers

Day has gone and the young couple walk out to look
at Mr. Moon.

"I wonder if the moon really is made of green cheese,"
he said. She answered, "maybe, but not the commodity
kind." They both laugh as he hands her a can of Indian
champagne.

He looked at her and said, "if I could reach up and grab
a handful of stars, I would sprinkle you with them so
they could shine on your beauty. Then every path you
walk will always be lit."

She said, "every path I walk, you will be beside me.
You are my stars, my sun and my moon."

He pops another can of beer, pulls off the ring and
hands it to her. "Until I can make you a better one will
you accept this ring?" "Yes! Yes!" she said as she
embraced him.

Then they both snuggle under the blanket and look at
the moon. Both lost in this moment of love, not
knowing that they have been rewarded by the moon
with a memory to last a life time.

Mr. Moon you are the greatest aphrodisiac of all time.

Rookie in Love

She told me she found another love. My whole body ached with the pain of loss. I was just a rookie in love.

I was twelve years old, but could feel the pain of loss to a jock who will leave her next week.

     I was dateless.

Would she want to come back to me? Probably. But I would tell her to go back to the jock.

In the meantime, I soothed my broken heart knowing her body ached just as mine did.

Now that I am older and an expert in the ways of love, girls will line up to be with me. Each wanting to dance with me and hold my hand.

     Damn!

It feels good to be fifteen.

Will I Carry Your Last Name?

Did I want to carry your last name?
     Not at first.
Too many roads to travel, too many people to meet.
I had a lot of living to do as a single person.

Will you disappear from my life and become extinct?
Will you cry for me and be sad?

A voice inside of me calls out….
     "Foolish Girl,
how can you be so blind? You will lose him."

Yes! I will choose to carry your name.
This kind of love may never come again.

We can meet new people, and travel new roads
together. Sometimes without maps and get lost.
     Who cares?

We will have more dreams to become a reality together,
more mysteries to solve together.

We will dance and laugh together in the rain.

We will do it all with the same name.

Indian Love Call

Bert and Millie, a native couple, were together for many years. In the evening Bert would play his flute and Mille would sit and listen while they sat under an arbor.

One day Millie passed over to the other side and Bert was devastated with grief. He did nothing but sit and grieve.

One evening Bert took his flute to the arbor, sat down and played his flute. He saw Millie walking up the road toward him. He kept playing and Millie sat down and listened to him.

After he stopped playing, Millie left. The woman with the sad eyes but still with a full heart of love for Bert.

After that, whenever Bert would play his flute, Millie would come and listen. A love call for her from Bert.

One day Bert's flute was silenced forever. He went over to join Millie on the other side. He was no longer a lonely soul who walked a dusty road alone. They were reunited.

Sometime in the evening when the wind is blowing, you could almost swear it was the sound of a flute.
Bert still serenading Millie. Happy at last.

When Love Dims

When you say wicked words to someone,
it darkens your image.

When you speak to someone in a hostile
manner, the radiance that once shown
around you will dim.

It will darken so much that they will never
see you again.

Friends that you once had will pass you
on the street and not even see you.

So watch what you say. Your mouth may
dim every light in your life.

Teton Sioux
after Bodmer

My Moccasins

I walked in the way of darkness in my moccasins for so long.

Now they are old and worn.

It hasn't been an easy life with you. Such anger and abuse.

Tomorrow at first light of day, these moccasins will walk away from you forever.

You will eat alone, sleep alone and live alone. Loneliness Is a deep ditch to climb out of.

These moccasins will take me back to the tribe in which I am a member.

I will not be alone. My days of walking in darkness is over. Yours is just beginning.

Eventually I will get a new pair of moccasins and be joyfully happy, but I will keep the old.

Perhaps make a pair for my first granddaughter, and tell her the many stories of the past yesterdays of these worn moccasins.

Potpourri

I Hear Dreams

I hear dreams. Some are loud and imposing.
These I can do without.

Some are sad and some are happy and not so bad. I hear
crying in a sad dream and laughter
in a happy dream.

I wake up crying in a sad dream, but I don't wake up
laughing in a happy dream.

Loud dreams awaken me when they talk too loud.
Continuous talking.

On and on.

I will have to muffle them some way.

How do you muffle a dream?

In Another Lifetime

Did I pass you on the street? Was I looking
the other way, as you were picking up something
you dropped?

If I was only five seconds slower, I would have
reached down and picked up your item for you.
A missed opportunity of five seconds to meet one
another.

I don't know if we were meant to be together
In this lifetime. If so, sometime in the future we
will meet when it is meant to be.

If not. See you in the next lifetime.

Trees Walk Among Us

Trees walk among us
> Like soldiers, up the mountains as if they are
> climbing to reach the very top to be nearer
> to God. On river banks, in parks as well as
> hiking trails that bring beauty into our lives.

Trees walk among us
> As well as the birds and other creatures to
> provide us with a shaded place to obscure
> and intercept the rays of sun and protect
> our bodies.

Trees walk among us
> Do they scream out in pain and anguish
> when someone carves their name into their
> skin? I hope not.

Some trees no longer walk among us
> They did not make the journey. They wither
> away, dried and shriveled up with limbs that
> are broken and ragged... reaching out to be
> rescued.

Trees walk among us
> like the people in our lives who's journey
> ends when it's their time to go. They reach
> out their hand for one last goodbye.

The Fog

Lying here awake in the middle of the night
I hear the lonesome sound of a fog horn in the
distance.

Looking out the window at the fog wondering
what it hides. A robbery, a murder, or just a
lonesome being going home to an empty house.

A group of kids stopping at a diner for breakfast
after a night of partying. Ah! Sweet youth,
enjoy it while you can. Someday you may be the
one who lies awake at night and hears the
lonesome sound of a fog horn, wondering where
did my youth go?

Dammit! Why do the years go by so fast? Why
can't the vigor of youth last a little longer?

I hear the fog horn again. Wish I could get to
sleep.

Can't wait for the hustle and bustle daylight brings.

Were You an Angel?

I saw you standing beside the bed.
You with your yellow hair and dazzling smile.
Were you an angel? Perhaps! A hallucination, I think
not. You had no wings and no shirt, but a glow of light
encircled you and made for an impressive grandee.

I was frightened. Who were you and what were you
there for? I shut my eyes and when I opened
them you were gone.

 Were you there to bless our union which was only
two weeks old? Were you there to tell my brain, be
happy and love all who love you.

I never saw you again, but feel your presence when it is
quiet and my eyes are closed.

I wish I knew your name. Maybe whisper it in my ear
someday. After all, you did visit me and I feel we are old
friends.

I would like to see you again and converse with you.

I'm guessing you still look the same.

Angel? Spirit guide? A friendly ghostly existence?
For whatever reason your visit, I hope I have lived
up to your expectations and then some.

Mother Earth

We have been raping mother earth for too long. She is screaming loud and jerking because of the pain. The earth trembles and shakes causing death to thousands and destroying their way of life.

The ocean is a cesspool not fit to eat what comes out of it, nor to swim in it. The air is brown and filthy and causes illness in the old and very young. We will never be free from fear and we will continue to experience anxiety.

Fear because we had eyes, but did not see, ears but we did not listen. Now we are overwhelmed with earthquakes, tsunamis, and air that is unfit to breathe.

Mother earth will continue to rumble and fight back. We have ignored her for too long and she will punish us all.

The birds will cease to sing. We will be unable to grow crops to feed ourselves and have clean drinking water.

We will be like the continent of Atlantis and collapse into ocean, be covered with water and never ever to be seen or heard of again.

Then we will all sleep for eternity.

Stranger in a Strange Land

The earth was created the day I was born. Strange
things spring out of the ground and embrace me in their
limbs. Fruit for food and leaves to cover me. The falling
of water from the sky that fills every hole and valley to
form the sea and lakes, filled with fish and other sea
creatures. A stream of water to drink.

I pick up some stones and throw them up to the sky.
They keep going and become bright and sparkle down on
me...stars.

Now, I am a stranger in a strange place. Are there others
out there? Am I not to be in the company of others? I
am a crazy loner in a strange land. The tension inside of
me screams out in pain. Solitude can be hard to accept.

Then I see a door and a man walks through it. "Is your
imagination playing tricks on you again he asks? Take
this pill and it will ease the burden on your delusion."
Ah yes! The little white pill that will make me normal.

I knock the pill out of his hand, run through the door,
down the hall and out the door. I keep running. If this is
normal I don't want to live in a world where you are
mocked because of the color of your skin, where people
are hungry and living on the street. Crime, so very much
crime.

All of a sudden I am in the strange land again. With birds singing, and sun shining. I sit down and catch my breath. I would rather be in solitude in this world then in the other world with a lock on the door.

Yes! I am finally living in a normal world.

I report to no one except my Creator.

While Loneliness Speaks to Me

Sitting here alone trying to draw or write. Where
is everybody? Will this loneliness ever subside? Or will I
continue this downward spiral into the well of
deprivation where other depressed beings reside?

The songs playing "oldies but goodies" don't help.
They only increase the sadness and difficulty I feel
in trying to concentrate and think.

Perhaps if I throw this ash tray across the room and it
makes a hole in the wall. What is wrong with me? Now I
am thinking of destroying my property.

Can't have a cigarette, doctor said it wasn't good
for me...neither was his bill. Can't play cards,
except solitaire which I hate. Even the leaves that roll
across the patio are more than one. The birds all flock
together.

Ah! Loneliness! I once welcomed you into my life
so I could get some rest and work done. Now I will leave
the door open and hope you leave and never return. I
won't keep the light on after your departure.

Perhaps if I get some sleep, the friends and relatives who
went before will come and visit. I will then not be alone.
Crazy perhaps, but not alone.

I Walk Through This World Alone

I walk this world alone. Passing people on the
street with empty faces. No smiles and with eyes
that look through you as if you don't exist. An
invisible being.

I walk through this world alone. How many other
neglected beings walk in this bleakness of despair
called loneliness?

I walk through this world alone in a population
that refuses to acknowledge a fellow entity
who has a real heart and soul? A heart that
feels pain and a soul that longs to be wanted.

Back in my room I sit alone. The curtain of
darkness covers my windows. Shall I sit in the
darkness alone? Or in the lighted room alone?

Doesn't matter. No one cares. After all I am
alone. One of those individuals destined to
walk through this world alone.

The Wind

Today someone died...how do I know? The wind told me so. The wind went sailing through the night like the unsubdued turmoil of wind and rain. She was old and sick. Death was a welcome occurrence for this person.

Today a flower died...how do I know? The wind said so. This fragrant fragile blossom cried a little as it gasped its last breath and wilted away.

Today someone was born...how do I know? A dove flew by my window and told me so. All of the birds chirped in unity for this welcome event.

Another being entering the human race to survive and exist until the wind comes forcefully sailing through the night and whispers that someone has died.

Yes! Today someone died, and another was born. A flower wilted and another was planted.

This closed curve called a circle, the circle of life which all of us must experience...from birth, through our life span, to the certainty of death.

I was hoping God would make an exception in my case.

The wind wouldn't tell me that.

Tell Me Kind Sir

I look at the reflection in the mirror. The once smooth, carefree smiling face, is now grey and gaunt with lines that go in all directions. Somewhat like a map that goes on and on.

Was it yesterday I was going to learn how to deep sea dive or back pack thru Europe? Now this back of mine has this unpleasant sensation that tells me "No."

The anguish and agony of becoming a senior isn't what I envisioned. Arthritic hands, eyes that can barely see, spasmodic feet.

Can I order another skin, another back? How did this happen? I went to bed one day, a youth full of piss and vinegar, and woke up a miserable antiquated individual.

Looking at the clock seeing every second pass only makes me more depressed. The movement of time is too rapid. In the blink of an eye...days, months, years move too quickly.

Can I have a second chance of youth? I promise not to waste it this time. "No!" says the all-knowing mind, "You had your time."

Tell me kind sir, can you point me the way to hell, or am I already there and don't know it? If this isn't hell...
then pray tell, what is it?

Feeling Insecure

Feeling insecure as the last leaf on a tree that will fall on the ground of a layer of snow.

My head hurts, and my heart aches. Like a fog that hovers over me and won't leave.

How did I get this way? Was it because someone called me dumb? Did they make fun of my appearance?

If I only can get these feet to move and this body to follow.

Suddenly a scream escapes from my throat and mouth. Insecurity can be hell.

I think Instead I will sit here in this chair, close my eyes and see nothing but insecurity in my future.

Death Is Like Time in A House.

Children are in the kitchen eating cereal, laughing and happy.

After lunch a teenager in the den playing with an X-box while another is listening to music on an I-pod.

The day passes...
Then young adults having dinner with mom and
dad in the dining room. One child home from
college and the other visiting from another state.

My how time flies in this house...
Then up the stairs to go to bed...happy to be together
once more in the same house.

The next morning with one less person...
Did he slip out during the night without saying
good-by? Was his need for solitude so great he
moved on?

No!
He has left the house for good. Death came in the night
and took him away to God in Heaven where his spirit will
live forever.

Now the house stands empty. The memories
bring a cracking sound of sadness to the house
of what was once a happy home.

Buffalo Robes

The sky is blue and the sun is warm.
I get my bow and arrow. A good day for hunting.

I bring down a bison. Others help to bring it to the
campsite.

Tonight we will feast and sing songs to the Creator
who provides for us.

We will all go to bed full and happy. Not knowing what
tomorrow will bring.

Maybe a rain storm. Worse! A run in with the enemy.
The ones with hair on their faces. The ones who
slaughter the bison for their skins and let the meat rot.

The bison have become scarce. We have had fights with
the ones with the ones who slaughter. After all we have
children who need to eat.

But our bow and arrows are no match for the long stick
with the loud noise that they carry.

Since the bison has become scarce, maybe they will
move on, leave us alone and take their skins with fleas
with them.

I Grabbed These Words Just for You

I am like a writer who grabs words out of the air and throws them onto a page hoping they make sense to the reader.

Words to entertain and others to educate.

There are so many words floating around the air near me. Some I touch and they break. Others I feel electricity.

I grab more words. The other words made no sense. How can I be sure which words to grab?

I start grabbing words and throwing them down, page after page.

Now I grab some for the title.

"Reading for Dummies"

I don't think so. Probably won't sell.

"Happiness Is a Hand Full Of Words"

Like it. Makes sense to me.

So grab some words and happy reading to all.

The Whistle of the Wind

The wind blows a tune of loneliness tonight.

I lie here wondering why I am here.

Certainly not to discover a cure for a disease. I don't know chemistry.

I don't want to be the first female president. Or the second or the third. Regardless of what I do, it will never be good enough.

Don't want to be an astronaut and go to other planets. I like this one just fine.

Don't want to be a chef. Don't care too much for food. Gordon Ramsey need not worry.

I will just lie here and listen to the wind whistle his tune of loneliness.

A solitary existence is not for me.

This Band of Heroic Angels Over There

Not playing a harp on a floating cloud.

They are over there on the battlefield. The sadness
on their faces as they lift a soul out of a lifeless body.
A brave soul whose unseeing eyes and silent breath will
never see his loved ones again.

Some of the young men are scared and crying. Angels
are flying all over the battlefield and wrapping their
wings around the soldiers. They will be protected from
the grenades and other artillery. The young men can
say when they go home, that they were protected on
the battlefield by an angel.

But they shed tears for their fallen brothers who will
not make it back home again. Is this the way peace is
won?

But wait!

I see a NEW band of heroic angels over there. Angels I
recognize on a personal basis. My fallen brothers have
been raised to a higher level to protect other brothers
in battle.

This band of heroic angels over there.

Woman in Red Dress

There you sit in your red dress with stars on the
sleeves and shell beads on your chest.

Your hair is long and braided and your forehead rouged.

Why is your back to the window? Is there something
outside you do not wish to see or do you want to
look at me looking back at you as you tighten your
leather belt.

Who served as the model for you in all your beauty?

Woman in The Window

Someone who sat with stoic face and noble soul.

They captured you in all your beauty.

Now you hang on the wall in all your beauty as a work
of art.

Looking at me as I look at you.

Woman in The Window

Why Wasn't I Born a Man

No more hairdressers twice a week. No more talking
and wondering If she is listening. Clip Clip, Snip Snip.
Perhaps a grunt every now and then. Why do I put up
with it? Because women are so vain.

If I were born a man: a haircut every three weeks, maybe
worry about the bald spot in the back. Don't care if the
barber is listening or not.

I could belch without someone looking at me as though I
committed a sin. I could scratch myself all I want
without being given the evil eye.

     Not so a woman.

If I were born a man: I could fall asleep on the couch
with my mouth open and snore so loudly, that the
neighbors come out to see if a bear wondered into their
yard.

If I were born a man: I could eat pizza and chili dogs and
not have to worry if it will go to my hips. I would not
worry if my belly gets so large that it protrudes over my
belt.

If I were born a man: I would not go shopping and try on
everything in the store and still walk out with nothing
because I didn't find anything I liked. Instead I would go

in the store, grab a tee shirt, a pair of jeans pay for them and walk out of the store without trying them on.

If I were born a man: I would not have to go out and have a salad with the girls. Instead I would go out for a beer and shoot pool with the guys, get drunk and not worry about women hitting on me thinking I am easy because I drank too much. That happens to women a lot.

I could go to a public bathroom alone. I can't imagine asking another man if he would like to go to the bathroom with me. Not so women. I really don't know why they always go together. I would not have to stand in the line that never seems to move. Instead I can go in and be out in five minutes.

If I were born a man: I would not have to go through the nightly sweats and crying jags when I reach forty. True I would have to be on the receiving end and be careful of what I say, otherwise Niagara Falls

If a man goes grey, he looks distinguish. A lady, most of the time thinks she looks old. Not always but most of the time. Would I look good in grey? I don't think so. I would look old.

Yes! men have all the luck.
    Bless their hearts.

My Shadow

Sometimes I look at my shadow and reach out to touch it but It moves on.

Shadows can be lost, especially at night. Even Peter Pan lost his shadow. Windy had to sew it back on.

Sometimes I run after it but it seems to elude me like certain things in life elude me. Talent, natural thinness...physical beauty.

A young man I once knew left his shadow on my heart. That shadow I can feel. The anguish of heartbreak. I have no need to chase it. It feels dark and silent.

Shadows can be something lost or vanished, like a lost love or a sunset that vanishes at dawn.

Shadows can be frightening, especially at night. When you see another shadow standing beside you, or when you see the shadows of a tree branch at your window and think that someone is at your window.

I do not like you shadow, why do you bother me? You leave me alone in the night, but when daylight comes you are there once more. Sometimes taller then I, sometimes at my feet, depending on the light that hits my body.

I keep chasing shadows knowing that some things cannot be so easy to grasp. It can be abnormal, even demented to chase shadows, but I like challenges.

I consider it a challenge to try to grasp my shadow; after all it is always with me.

I wouldn't know what to do with my shadow if I caught it. Throw it away, stand on it and become its shadow? That would be Interesting.

Perhaps I will stop chasing my shadow one day and let It come along with me on life's journey.

Yes! Me and my shadow, the both of us together.

You Flow in and Out of my Life

Every day you are in my life coexisting without knowing morning, noon and night.

"How can I live without you? I can't!"

Your transparent, unique beauty and sometimes unpleasant presence can be majestic and imposing.

I never think of you before going to bed, but when I awaken, you are on my mind.

First you come to me, then you leave again. Perhaps rushing to foreign shores then, maybe, back again, seeing the beauty of the ocean and all that pleasures you.

A small mermaid riding a dolphin.
A sea horse on its way to a coral reef.

I envy the beauty that you have seen and the way that you supply the earth.

No, I cannot live without you. My life would be barren. I would hallucinate, dry up and wither away. Eventually I would give into that darkness that all must succumb to...Death.

So thank you for furnishing my life with your presence. My friend Mr. H20.

Elements

Storm clouds dark in the sky. Some black, some dark grey. Soon to cry on us in torrents of rain. Crying on the crops to make them grow, the humans on their way to work or home. Silently cursing this element that is needed to keep them alive.

Snowfall coming down covering the ground. The pattern of each snow flake, while different, is a thing of beauty that covers the ground like a white rug. A rug that cannot be duplicated.

The snowflakes make for beauty on the trees. The white snow mixed with the green of the evergreen make for a wondrous scene. Somehow, I am not cold.

I hear a soft knocking on my window. It's Mr. Sun in all his warmth and glory awakening me for another day.

I go for a walk in the warmth of the sun, listening to the creatures of summer all around. A bird, a squirrel or a waterfall. I so much enjoy this day.

Soon Mr. Sun will say good night. Tomorrow morning he will be at my window again, knocking and telling me to get up and enjoy the day.

Made in the USA
Columbia, SC
22 October 2021

47343841R00067